Mind, Body, and Spirit

Mind, Body, and Spirit

Poems about
Drugs
Feeling and Emotion
The ABC of School Sports
Analysis of Tomorrow

By

Larry W. McEachin

ISBN: 1-58721-209-9 (Paperback)

This book is printed on acid free paper.

Printed in the United States of America
First Printing, 1997

1stBooks – rev. 04/07/03

About the Book

This book would encourage and motivate a person. My book would make people feel good about themselves. It would make people aware of their environment and surroundings, and how to help out with the situation of things, in the way of communication, and how to get along with people. In my book, there are 44 poems about drugs, 27 poems about feeling and emotions, 18 poems about the analysis of tomorrow from different perspectives, 6 ABC of school sports. This book would help elevate the minds of people, and to communicate better with others.

Preface

This book was written by Larry W. McEachin, and his partner, the Holy Spirit.While reading Mind, Body and Spirit, the purpose is to help create a network of concern. This book will help give people more power in their life. The contents of this book include poems about drugs, feelings, emotions, the analysis of tomorrow, and the abc's of sports. This book would help start a network of concern, by strengthening the mind and making people view things in a positive manner. The message in this book will improve parent-child communications, and help get people on one accord. Mind, Body and Spirit speak on various topics of life, which relate to our way of being, our mental thoughts, and our spiritual well being. This book will help direct people away from doing harmful things, by encouraging them to deal with different situations in a positive manner. This book would encouraging and motivating a person's mind, body, and spirit. It will help improve life's situations and will make the environment better as a whole. This book will cushion the mind against evil thoughts and give aid and comfort to a person's life.

CONTENTS

Drugs

1

1. Drugs, the affect it have on people and society

There are much happen in this world, we are living in,
Much to say where peace, need to harper within.
Drugs affect a people standard, their normal way to be.
This cause uncertain for people, like you and me.
What happen to the world, where is the future going.
If drugs keep up, then the future would be ruin.
What happen to things, how did it get this way?
What happen that cause ruin, to the future of one's day?
This became an issue to people alone the years.
When illicit drugs came, made things more severes.
It affect ones judgement, one's way of being.
It cause blind spot, in one's way of seeing.
Illicit drugs has it affect on society, it way of thinking,
It affect society, even before morality start sinking.

2. Drugs, how it affect teens behavior

Drugs cause teen to do things, not so proud.
They act up, when they get involve with a crowd.
They get in a mood, they go to and fro.
They soon get to the place, they don't care where
    they go.
Drugs would cause people, to lie cheat and steal,
It affect their mind, it cut down on their will.
It put people in a stage, a question as to why.
The thing they look forward to, is their next high.
This is a serious matter, for one to get involve.
Why should one risk their life, to that resolve.
This is an addicted stage, for a person to be in,
It cause them to do deadly things, every now and
    then.

3. Drugs, its affect on people life

How must things go, for it to be like this?
Because of the affect of drugs, ones mind at risk.
The use of drugs, it destroy ones life.
To keep with the effort, bring on tension and strife.
Drugs have an affect in families, it cause them to
   scatter,
Because of the affect of things, it have on this
   matter.
Drugs is a costly thing, it tear the family apart,
They question themselves, how did it ever start.
From false impression, saying it a hip thing to get
   into,
One's find out the harsh reality, that not true.
It cause withdraw from life, what people normally
   do.
It affect other behavior, their dealing with them to.

5. Teens and the affect of drugs use

Drugs has a very harmful effect on teens of today.
It threaten their normal development, in a number of
    ways.
Drugs interfere with one's memory, their state of mind.
It cause affect to sensation, uncertain they would find.
Drugs distort experience and cause loss to be a toll.
It can user to harm themselves, and loose control.
Drugs interfere with the brain ability to take things in.
It cause information to be distorted from within.
Drugs mess with one perception, their way of seeing.
It mess up one life, their way of being.

6. Drugs discipline of right and wrong.

There is a sense of discipline, to know right from wrong,
To help instill the value, people need all along.
To set good example, a prescription to go by.
So something don't come up and a question as to why.
Drugs affect people behavior, their way of being.
It take away from understanding, their way of seeing.
Illicit drugs leave people in a bad condition.
Teach teens right from wrong, and stand by their
    conviction.
Looking at illicit drugs, the problem facing us today,
Must it continue on, for things to be that way.

7. Drugs the choice that we make

Drugs the choice in life, people make,
Does it do with what given, or that we forsake.
There a slogan to promote the ideal drugs free,
In a wholesome society, that the only way to be.
The topic and meaning, for things being like this,
It letting people know, their life is at risk.
This is not the meaning of life, for things to be like
    this.
There are other way to look, which give a motivating
    twist.
There a choice in life, that we would either make,
Does it be this way, or the other way we take.
The aim of life is the choice like this.
Messing with illicit drugs, put ones life at risk.

8. Drugs the assessment of things

Looking at drugs, the assessment, a matter of time,
Seeing the situation, the affect it have on crime.
Where do we go to take a closer look at things?
Do we see this matter, for what it eventually brings?
This is a cause for alert, a cause to worry about.
To help take care of the future, to help take care of
    the doubt.
Where is this world going how is the direction of
things?
How do we assess this matter, to see what good it
    brings?
This is a time of concern, a time to worry about.
A time to be aware, a time to be on the look out.
It take different program, and working together.
If not pity, to understanding this matter.

9. Description of a neighborhood, before and after drugs

There was a place, being a good neighborhood,
Things went along in it, the way it should.
A good place for children, a good place to live at,
Because of the manner of things, it was like that.
A close knit neighborhood, walking the street, a social
    event.
Because of the policy of drugs, that no longer the intent.
That no longer the case, drugs brought about a change.
This is not the quiet neighborhood, things not the same.
Things has change, not too many people walk the street.
Not many people in the neighborhood, one would meet.
Some people walk the street, without safety as a
    concern,
They take this matter lightly, for what need to be learn.

10. Drugs affect on a neighborhood

Whenever there come drugs, in a neighborhood,
It throw things out of bound, not going like it
should.
The old people stay inside, afraid to come out,
Afraid for their safety, how things may come about.
Afraid that a bullet may come through their window
at any time.
Because of the ideal of drugs, it association with
crime,
Too them things began, to seem like a war zone.
They are not by themselves, they are not alone.
People in the neighborhood became concern, they
talk things out.
They did not want this in the neighborhood, for
things to be about.
The fear of their action, did not mobilize them,
They ask for other help, to help make things less
dim.

11. City Council reaction of drugs in a neighborhood

The city council decided to rezone the area, that was their move.

They work for the interest of things, so the people would approve.

They were trying to help the nieghborhood, get rid of crime,

Working for the peace of things, in the interest of time.

The neighborhood has since change, drugs dealing going on,

This is not there kind of neighborhood, things are wrong.

People sometime cannot rest, they cannot sleep at night.

Because of what wrong in the neighborhood, that make things uptight.

They sometime take different route on their way home,

Because of the fear of things, how things may rome.

12. Drugs being a harmful thing

Illicit drugs is a harmful thing, to be on the street.
It have an affect on people, we sometime meet.
There is the talk, the concern of it being around.
Drugs cause heartache, it get things out of bound.
There is a drugs crisis, happen in our society today.
If this keep up, it would do harm to the future way.
In some places, its causing a plague in the
     neighborhood.
It not working in the interest of things, that is good.
Because of this, some people staying more in home
Drugs causing their neighborhood to become a
     combat zone.
This matter affect young people, their state of mind.
It not in their best interest, they would find.

13. The observance of drugs use

Parent need to be knowledgeable about the signs of
   drugs use.
To observe this matter, so their won't be abuse.
Drugs cause people in life to have ill affect.
It cause disorder, that get life upset.
People sometime hate themself, and do not care.
Because of drugs, ill affect is there.
The question one would ask, the biggest problem
   facing us today,
Drugs has the biggest affect on the future way.
It is a problem with an increasing growing concern.
It is a problem that affect society, and its mean to
   learn.

14. The deadly affects of drugs

It might bring on a high, for the time being,
What about the deadly affect, that way of seeing?
Children should be taught to resist such pressure as
    this.
That bring on such an affect, and put their life at
    risk.
There are peer pressure of drugs, brought on by
    other.
That would spread the ill affect of drugs to another.
There are help, to resist such pressure as this.
So it would not affect ones mind, and put their life at
    risk.
Friend play a very important part, in this matter,
For the supervision of things, that are not together.
Talk about one problem, their interest and things.
But stay away from drugs, because of deadly result it
    brings.

15. **Drugs and dependence**

Drugs cause physical and emotional dependence
User develop craving for it, which take away
    independence.
The affect of things, drugs bring about an increase.
The affect on life, it cause a decrease.
Drugs may lead to the increase of drugs use.
Because of that response, it cause drugs abuse.
Regular use of drugs, may develop a tolerance
    affect,
A larger dose is need for the same effect.
Drugs become very expensive, it cause ruin to one
    life.
To keep the habit going, cause tension and strife.
There are response of combining drugs, that bring
    devastating result.
There are also drugs hotline, that one can consult.

16. Drugs give a false security

Drugs give the user a false sense of functioning on
   their own.
It give a false security, and leave them alone.
Alone with their problem, and whatever facing them.
Life for the user, become harsh and very dim.
Drugs have cause response, to an increasing
   demand.
With this threat to society, will it ever end.
Different form, different method to produce things.
The aim of life, dissillusion is what it brings.
It need to be taught that drugs, is deadly wrong.
When one mess with drugs, their life is not their
   own.
There is a need to teach the standard of wrong and
   right.
If one mess with drugs, their life become uptight.

17. The beginning of drugs use

It start with a funny cigarettes, something like that,
Then other substance is tried, to see where things is
    at.
The first temptation of drugs, usually in a social
    situation.
From that point, there may be peer persuasion.
Making the statement, it a hip thing to do,
When it come to the harsh reality, that not true.
They are given false and inaccurate information,
Getting involve with drugs, because of the peer
    pressure situation.
Drugs from regular use, that continues to multiple
    use.
When it reach that point, that call drug abuse.

18. People caught up in drugs

People are caught up in the middle, young people
    involve.
A lot need to be done, for this matter, to be solve.
Their's a cheaper addiction of cocaine, known as
    crack.
Because of its cheapest, people keep coming back.
This is a serious form of drugs addiction.
Because of that way, more people are hook.
The question of drugs, what is the purpose of it.
Is it to help or cause bad benefit.
What can drugs do, in a family, and its matter?
Does it cause things, in the family to be scatter?

19. The affect of illicit drugs

Looking at the affect of illicit drugs, what it do,
Because of the harsh reality one life is through.
Some people are no longer with us, because of drugs.
They are no longer able, to walk on their family rugs.
They say to themself, that drugs was a hip thing to do.
It not only mess up their life, but the life of other to.
Illicit drugs interfere with ones life, their way of being.
It upset one sight, their way of seeing.
Among the casualties of drugs, are innocent people involve.
There are mishap in life, for this matter to be resolve.
There are victim of drugs, that has not been born yet.
Their's a lot of happen to this matter, that cause upset.

20. Illicit drugs in our society

Looking at illicit drugs in our society, it bring out
the ill.
A matter that need to stop, that slow down one will.
Illicit drugs, unnecessary need for it to be around.
It cause upset, it get people life, out of bound.
Looking at drugs, the situation confronting us today,
Is that how things going, toward the future way?
The process of illicit drugs, an illegal business is
that,
Because of how thing goes, it get life out of tact.
Looking at sign and wonder, the situation of the
crime,
If one get caught at it, they would sure do time.
Looking at the situation, and the way things is going,
That because of the affect, and how things is doing.

21. Illicit drugs, a concern for the future

Looking at illicit drugs, they are very much concern.
Not for it to affect the future, so they can learn,
People do not want their community tarnish by this.
Being aware of what might happen, it association
  with risk,
The question of these drugs, what is the good of it?
Is it taken for medicine, which provide good benefit?
Good drugs for one's health, help take care of
  sickness,
Illicit drugs as an agent, help bring out wickedness.
Drugs what is it good for, what the purpose of it.
Because of the lack of care, their's not much benefit.
With all the drugs around, what are we going to do.
Will it be use for wrong, or the way that is true.

22. Illicit drugs, what the good of it

The question of illicit drugs, what the good of it?
It narrow one's reason, it cause lack of benefit.
Illicit drugs sometime leave people in a bad way.
It cause upset, to the future of one's day.
Illicit drugs sometime leave people no way at all.
They are no longer able to hear people, when they
  call.
The question of these drugs, it assure crime.
If one get caught, they would sure do time.
People in some community, trying to do something
  about drugs,
They do not want this matter, swept under their rugs.
Being concern about the future, about what's going
  on,
They want to do right, so things won't be wrong.

23. With drugs, there is a problem in society

A drugs problem in the society, we are living in,
That make it harder for peace and harmony, to
    harvest within.
There is a education understanding, way with things.
How else can we see this matter, for understanding it
    brings?
The matter of illicit drugs, how can we asset this,
Because of the use of it, there are certain risk.
That because of illicit drugs, a wrong use for it.
It narrow one's compassion, it may cause fit.
Prescription drugs are use for differents things in
    life.
It help take care of the dealing of tension and strife.
Illicit drugs, there no good for it to be around,
It cause upset, and get people life out of bound.

24. Drugs what is the meaning of it

Drugs what is the meaning of it, what is this.
Is it the kind of stuff, that put people life in risk?
Is it the prescription drugs that are use?
Or is it the other drugs, that are abuse?
One is use for a medical purpose, which is a good
    call,
The other use for recreation, which is not good at all.
Drugs what is it, what are we talking about.
Is it something that help or put people life in doubt?
Drugs, is it the stuff, that be in a medicine chest?
Or is it the deadly substance, that people put to a
    test?
Trying to test for what gain, the high and the low,
Trying to see how far with things, they can go.

25. Drugs the consumption of it

It depend upon the use, the consumption of it.
To determine the aim of life, its benefit.
The wrong use of drugs, would mess up one life.
It would cause burden, which add to one's strife.
Is this world heading in the way of destruction?
Is there a need for development, a plan for
    construction?
Drugs, what is the price, that a person has to pay?
What will it do, toward the future of one's day?
Drugs the misuse of it, lead to destruction.
It tear up ones life and affect ones struction.
Drugs what is it good for, what does it do?
Proper use, provide relief to me and you.

26. Drugs what does it do?

Drugs what is it good for, what does it do?
The misuse of it, cause one life not to be true.
Where is this world going, where is it leading to.
With illicit drugs out there, what will we do.
There is a lot happen, there is a lot going on
Drugs interfere with the safety factor, for things to be wrong.
How do we asset this matter, how do we see it?
With illicit drugs in our society, it upset benefit.
There are stealing and worse things going on.
It add to the problem, that make things wrong.
Greater awareness then this, which take the toll of one life.
It create destruction, which bring on tension and strife.

27. With drugs, where is this world going

Where is this world going, is the question I ask?
Is this how things going, toward the future task?
This is a matter of troublesome and growning concern.
There need to be education, so the future can learn.
The President becoming increasing outspoken about this matter,
There are information from other places, being gather.
How do we handle it, a question we need to response to?
Do we continue this way, for something we need to do?
Drugs use for the good, there a lot of good in it.
If uses for the wrong, there is hazard benefit.
There are hazard and misuse of drugs going on.
For that way of looking, make life turn out wrong.

28. Drug use for the bad or good

Drugs can be uses for the bad or for the good.
It depend upon how it taken, whether like it should.
People using illicit drugs, have a tendency to overdue things.
Pushing this matter to the limit, harmful result it brings.
When using illicit drugs, they are not taking proper care.
Because of its use, death may soon be there.
The wrong drugs are taken, they are taken as much,
Because of one effort, it affect life as such.
Illicit drugs cut down on activity, one way of life.
It affect life alteration, toward tension and strife.
These things associated with drugs, in this day and time.
It affect the way of peace, which bring on more crime.

29. Drugs, a need to make the best choice

A need to make the choice, the best we know how.

We won't worry about the problem we see now.

There is a lot happen in life, a lot going on.

This add to the problem, for things to be wrong.

There is a question, that involve a decision for ourself.

Do we go the way that is right, or the way that is left?

There is a need to help life, to get things along the way,

To determine the outlook, the future of one day.

The choice of drugs free, is a cause for instruction.

It cut down on things, that lead to destruction.

It depend upon the outlook, the foundation that is laid,

Which determine the aim of life, how things is made.

30. A need to develop a drugs free society

There is a need to get things develop along the way,
So the word drugs free, be the choice of ones day.
There are things in life, that might control one's
    mind.
These substance and matter, one need not to find.
Matter of these nature, are drugs related as such.
It would do harm to one life, no telling how much.
There is a decision, a choice in life we make.
Will the effort be drugs free, or the other way we
    take?
There is the saying, we get out of life what we put
    in.
Which determine the aim of life, how things are
    within.

31. Drugs interfere with safety

The thought of safety on the job, a prime concern.
It made in the effort, so the people money, they can
earn.
The thought of drugs, the way of it ill affect.
It cause things to happen, that get things upset.
Drugs is getting to be sidespread, in a variety place.
It interefer with safety, that lead to disgrace.
It would interefer with the way of life, and its
success.
Drugs cause things to happen, that cause things to
regress.
The talk of drugs testing at the workplace,
Its done in the effort, in order to make things safe.
A need for a good job, to keep things up to par,
So a good relationship in the workplace, be better by
far.

32. The deterioration that drugs cause

Drugs would cause deterioration, to the success of
   things.
It hamper one effort, is the result it brings.
There is a test for drugs, in a person blood stream,
If things are positive, it may affect their dream.
The thought of job performance, would be a
   concern.
Drugs may affect their health, as one may learn.
There are the concern of other, at the workplace.
It done for the effort, in order to make things safe.
It done for the health of people, as things would
   involve.
It done for job safety, so problem would be solve.

33. The report card on drugs

The report on drugs, are in the process of being in.
How are the war on drugs, being fought within.
The time is here, the grade is incomplete.
There are things to talk about, as one would repeat.
Different opinion clash, with similiar points of view.
How is this war being fought, for things to be true?
There are a lot to be done, from a certain perspective.
Are things being put in place, to meet the objective.
There are different opinion, and different point of view.
There are need for money, for things to be true.
Education need to be sharping, to bring things in tact.
Because it equal important to deal with knowledge and fact.

34. Drugs, an important matter facing us

This is an important matter, facing us here.
What will we do, before things get more severe?
In dealing with this, we must make people relize,
This is a deadly matter, that need to subside.
There is a need to have a understanding of this matter.
So drugs in this country, would not become scatter.
The extent of drugs is a problem, that is happen as such.
It is happen in society, it is happen so much.
It going to take work, and a lots of time,
To help take care of drugs, and to reduce crime.
It did not happen overnight, for things to get this way.
The problem would not be solve overnight, nor the next day.

35. The continuing use of drugs

If one do not get off drugs, they would stay on it.

It would affect one behavior, death may be the benefit.

Prolonged use become part of the body chemistry being,

When regular user stop, withdrawal affect their seeing,

The body experience physiological trauma, things like that.

That not a good assetment, for one to be at.

These things occur, when drugs become the center of a user life.

Saying no to drugs, would take care of this tension and strife.

It destroy the unity of family being together,

It affect one interest and cause things to be scatter.

36. Instilling responsibility of drugs understanding

Because of society, its way of looking at things.
Value must be instill, for the best result it brings.
There is the teaching of the standard, right and
   wrong,
For the promotion of good, as time go along.
The teaching that drugs is bad, there is no good
Unless its use for medicine, like it should.
This is a drugs crazy society, we are living in,
It do not promote harmony for peace to happen
   within.
There is a need to be trouble, by what going on.
To do what right, and not be affect by the wrong.
Children need to have value, for the understanding
   of things,
To be aware of illicit drugs, bad result it brings.

37. Programs, to fight against drugs

There are program out, to help fight against this.
So drugs won't affect young people, and put their
    mind in a twist.
Drugs in our society, the affect it have on teen,
If things keep like this, it would affect their dream.
In some places, drugs has taken root,
It done for the sake of money, which nickname is
    loot.
Because of this, crime has risen to an increase.
A need to hamper things, so crime would decrease.
This is a booming business, the body count on the
    rise,
It time for a change, so their won't be no surprise.
There are reports on the answer, how things have
    been,
There are question to the reason, will there be an
    end.

38. None cooperation of drugs

In drugs, none cooperation, not to what a person is
doing,
Not to cooperate in anyway, that would add to life
ruin.
Cooperate in the way to give insight, and to
understand.
So concern for this matter, would not get out of
hand.
If it take locking up, whatever represent that.
That what need to be done, how things be at.
The use of illicit drugs, they are not taking proper
care.
Because of its use, death may soon be there.
Seeing this matter, the effect it have on crime,
If one get caught, the effect is death or time.

39. The debate on the drugs situation

There is a debate in this world, to built more institution.
It would take more than this, toward a lasting solution.
There is the promotion of the ideal of drugs, to say no,
There must be a understanding, so people know where to go.
There is a need to improve drugs education in all grades.
Through this effort, the improve of things would be made.
This matter need to be look at, it need to be supervise,
To see if things are on the decrease or on the rise.
The report card on drugs, how would we look at that,
Would it be determine by education, for things to be at.

40. The talk of legalizing drugs

A need not to give up the fight against illegal drugs.
This is an important matter, not to be swept under
the rugs.
It getting to the point, things getting out of hand.
It causing a lots of uncertain, it cause illegal
demand.
There are people, who talking about legalizing it.
How would this help, What would be the benefit?
Legalization would not prevent illegal sales of drugs
and crimes,
It would not happen that way, not in this day and
time.
This would not help drugs addicter, but so much.
They would continue their activity as of such.
Drugs would cause addicter to steal and kill.
It cut down on their morality, which affect their will.

41. Legalize drugs, an outrageous request

There have been answer to a number of questions,
How drugs sales would work, causing outrageous
    suggestion?
Looking at the message, it would sent to the younger
    one.
How would society work, how would it be done?
This is saying to drugs addiction, that it is approve.
Society would be affected, by that kind of move.
What would this do for society, what would be the
    affect?
This would do harm to society, and cause upset.
Legalized drugs would not cause an end to drugs
    related crime.
It would only cause more confusion, in this day and
    time.
The question is do drugs addicter get drugs not to
    get sick,
Or do these people get drugs just to have a kick.

42. The affect of legalizing drugs

To legalize drugs would not help things as such.
It would affect society, just that much.
It would cause society to loose it foundation,
Because of the structure of things, this profound situation.
The question one would ask, where is society going,
With this as the task, wouldn't society be ruin.
Drugs cause enough problem in this world already,
If that be the case, wouldn't things be more unsteady.
This would affect the nation and it economy.
It would cause kid to act up and become anonymous.
Drugs have an affect on crime, its way to be.
There are other ways, for people to look and see.
It would upset the way of life, for morality sake.
It would upset structure, and cause things to brake.

43. Leaders and the anti-drugs cartel

The President and other leaders, talking about this
matter,
On the issue of drugs, information need to be gather.
Talking about what need to be done, what they can
do,
Talking about this matter, seeking a new point of
view.
Their way is a drugs summit, this way with thing,
Trying to discuss the situation, to see what it bring.
They are working to get an anti-drugs cartel set,
Trying to see how far with this matter they can get.
They are discussing stragery and different point of
view,
Each trying to response for their own, what they can
do.
They are preparing to answer to the future call,
Hoping to get rid of this matter, so it won't affect us
all.

44. The first anti-drugs cartel

This is the first anti-drugs cartel, by leader ever,
Working for the future, so drugs would be never.
They are working, trying to stop the flow of drugs,
Trying to keep this matter, from getting under the
future rugs.
They form a close coordination, to agree on this
matter,
So drugs would not affect the future, and it being
scatter.
The war on drugs, would take different procedure
and thing,
It would take working together, for the best result it
bring.
Each country in their territory, involving force of
their own.
They have similar understanding, they are not alone.

45. A plan for drugs action

The plan for action of drugs, we need to take a look.
How do we go about this, is it by the book?
The entire community, schools need to be involve.
It would take everybody, for this matter to be resolve.
The parent have a leading role, they have to play,
The student are to learn the rules, and then obey.
This involve the entire community, religious group too.
There are social agencies, something for them to do.
The law enforcement, have things on its hand,
Because of the use of drugs, and its demand.
There are media attention given to this matter,
Talking about the issue of drugs, how things may be scatter.
Transmitting the message, saying that drugs is wrong,
Letting them know of life expected, how life get gone.

Feeling And Emotion

1. Adore

Adore is the admiration shown toward one another,
which treat them in the form of sister and brother.
Treating them with love according to the way one act,
getting an understanding of things that are in tact.
Treating them in the way of kindness and respect,
because of how things goes there's no reject.
There is the concern that a person may go about,
looking at things in the way where there's no doubt.
To worship a person in the way that is divine,
to treat them with respect in a way that is fine.
To have high regard for a person, their way of being,
to help a person in life, another way of seeing.
This would help a person in the way of delight,
to show kindness and love, this way that is right.
It would add to the statement that brings love in one's life,
is for a man to say he adores his wife.
Adore is to have high regards for a person or thing,
to work in the best interest that it bring.
Adoring makes it easy for a person to be with one another,
because of the high regards shown to the other.

2. Agitate

Agitate is to stir up, to cause things to get out of
    hand,
to cause upset, which makes life hard to understand.
it cause an angry expression on a person face,
it can lead to no good, which leads to disgrace.
It's a person trying to upset another person life,
it can lead to tension, which leads to strife.
It would stir up a person emotional way of being,
it would cause distrubance in their way of seeing.
It would cause shake up in the normal way with
    thing
it would hamper success, ill feeling it would bring.
An agitator getting on one's nerve, may cause harm,
doing things in a way that would cause alarm.
Agitation would cause hardship, it would lead to
    confliction,
it would add up, it may cause affliction.
Looking at life, the trouble coming from these sort
    of things,
looking at the situation, troubled results it brings.
Agitate cause a person to feel angry or bad,
It causes things to work in the way that is sad.

3. Bad

Bad is a person doing bad, with no good in it,
it's something that cause harm and affect benefit.
This is a person or thing represented in a bad way,
would do things that cause harm to the future of one
day.
This would affect a person in this day and time,
it would lead to the alter conclusion which is crime.
This would hamper success, and cause things to go
bad,
it would mess up ones' future, which makes things
sad.
When things are bad, there is no good involve,
that would mess up success for things to be solve.
When things are unpleasant, that represents a bad
way of being,
that affects everybody that's close in this way of
seeing.
When a person is wicked, there is no good in it,
they may turn out in the way of having a fit.
We need to be careful about things in this day and
time,
be careful of our actions that may lead to crime.
Bad represent a bad feeling, a bad way of being,
it causes upset in one's life, their way of seeing.
When a person is angry, irritable in a bad way,
that is cause to be a hinder to the future of one day.

4. Concern

Concern is showing cooperation and care toward one
  another,
that's like showing understanding, sharing the safety
  f others.
That happens through others, a concern for one well
  being,
to show an understanding, share what they are
  seeing.
We are to show understanding in a similar way,
to seek for understanding and the peace of one day.
This represent showing concern for one way of
  being,
to show a better understanding for one way of
  seeing.
When a person find someone in a certain way, a
  certain state,
they are to act in the interest of things before it's too
  late.
Concern is showing understanding, hoping things
  work out
it showing common feeling and interest without a
  doubt.
Trying to console that individual, making life better
  for them,
hoping for the best outcome, so life won't be dim.
It represents cooperation toward the same way with
  things,
looking at things in the effort for the result it brings.

5. Delight

Delight represent doing something good in a pleasing way,
doing something to bring out the happiness of one day.
It represent working for good, working for things that please,
doing things in a way that make things at ease.
It also represent that which gives joy to others,
doing things good for your sisters or brothers.
Some would say they are having delight, that time of day,
which shows peace and contentment as being the way.
Sometime giving a toy brings delight in a child's life,
that would help take care of uncertain and strife.
Sometime a person to another can bring that person delight,
because of how they go about things that make thing right.
Delight is the way that shows care and concern,
it enhance things in the way that people would learn.
It brings about a certain feeling, a certain way of seeing,
it helps one in life toward their way of being.
It helps make things go along in a better way,
it takes tension out of work, and enhance play.
It help attitude, putting a person in a good state of mind,
and take away difficult that makes things hard to find.

6. Desperation

Represent a person that acts in a desperate state of
    mind,
they make things harder in the way that cause
    decline.
A person act in a hurry, they act without a care,
they would be in that state of mind, no matter who's
    there.
It give the appearance that would cause harm to
    come about,
it happen in a way that cause things to be in doubt.
It brings about a fear that make it harder to be
    around,
because of how things go, don't know how things is
    bound.
When a person get that way, they try to hurry things
    through,
when one act that way, it's harder for things to be
    true.
When a person reach that point, it's not good to be
    around,
because of the uncertain that cause up and down
There are uncertain in life that may come about,
this is a state of altitude that would create doubt.
This is something that cause confusion from time to
    time,
this is also something that may lead to crime.
What are something that may come from this,
it would hamper ones' life that may cause risk.
This is a time to look out, a time to worry about,
this is something to look at that would cause doubt.

7. Disturbance

Disturbance is something that come about that cause
    strife,
it happen in a way that affect ones' life.
It would affect one way, ones state of mind,
it would make things hard to come by, even hard to
    find.
It puts things in a certain way, for people like you
    and me,
because of the way of life that's how things may be.
It puts a person in a mood, because of how things
    may come about,
it puts them in a state of mind that causes doubt.
People sometime do things that is disrespectful to
    other,
they sometime cause harm to their sister or brother.
Disturbance sometime cause pain and sorrow,
it makes a person feel like there is no tomorrow.
One must look at things for what it mean,
and not to look at things the way it seem.
When there is disturbance, there is no discipline
    involve,
because of the understanding that make things
    harder to solve.
It cause grief, it give people something to worry
    about,
it cause hardship that often leads to doubt.

8. Ecstasy

Being joyful, looking at the situation at hand,
following the order of things that fit the demand.
It bring on the feeling of receiving a great toy,
because of that feeling, there is the feeling of joy.
It represent thrill in life that may come about,
it represent a way that may bring on a shout.
This is a indication that bring things in delight,
it brings on a feeling that make things seem right.
It come in different forms, different ways with
    things,
it help one altitude, for better results it brings.
As we look at this matter to see how things transpire,
it brings about a change and not a question as to
    why.
Ecstasy represents a moment or occasion that come
    about,
it represents things in the fullest of working out.
This is the enchantment of life for things to be this
    way,
this is a great preparation that it take to make one
    day.
A strong feeling or joy of some kind,
which show the true delight that one would find.

9. Enrage

Enrage represents frustration and tension that come about,
it mess up ones' day, is how things work out.
It involve the kind of disturbance that make a person mad,
it make things turn out in the way that is sad.
Enrage represent a strong feeling of ill will,
it's a part of madness that bring on chill.
A way of expression represented by a negative emotion,
it represented in a way where there is no devotion.
A person shows a mad expression, how mad they may be,
this represent a negative way for people like you and me.
Enrage express things in the way of sorrow,
when that happens, it seems like there's no tomorrow.
This would take a toll on a persons state of mind,
it get things out of sort and cause things to get behind.
People lose touch with reality, what they suppose to do,
because of how things happen, fear will come through.
It cause grief and uncertain in life, that come about,
because of the hostility, it brings on more doubt.
Enrage is a way of madness, that affect one life,
it is the mood of behavior that bring on strife.

10. Friendship

Friendship is the liking of kindness shown to other,
to do things in the frame work like sister and brother.
It represent kindness and respect to other,
and not to deal with things in the way that is a bother.
Showing understanding and the similar aspect of things,
to work for the best, for good result it brings.
Friends mostly share a common understanding of thing,
they join in group participation, even to sing.
It is on this occasion that people share with one another,
working for the good of things and for each other.
They gain an understanding, a sense of ones' well being,
they help one another out in their way of seeing.
Friendship is usually on a good note, for things to go that way,
it does not always go in the best manner one would say.
They start out with good intention, with that thought in mind,
because of certain difficult, some things get left behind.
Friendship is someone who enables a friend along the way,
to give a better out look toward the future of one day.
How are friends easy to come by in this day and time,
it's a little more difficult, because things are not that prime.

11. Frustration

Is the mood a person gets in, that affect their state of
    mind,
it causes uncertainty in their life, they would find.
They'll be trying to do something for things to work out,
it brings on uneasy, which causes certain doubt.
Trying to figure things out, trying to get it the right way,
with frustration involve, this causes confusion to one
    day.
Things is at odd, things are out of place,
it gets to the point where it causes disgrace.
This is the point in time when things get up tight,
reaching that point when it enhance wrong and not right.
This is the moment in time when things reach that point,
it is at that time in life things seems out of joint.
Frustration make things seem confused and out of place,
it makes it harder to do things and harder to face.
Frustration will keep a person from doing things when
    they won't,
because of the misuse of the word meaning don't.
A person can be frustrated at what somebody's doing,
because of how such matters go that may cause ruin.
It depend upon how things is applied in ones' life,
which has something to do with the way of ones' strife.

12. Glad

Is an expression of good, which may come about,
which take care of the dealing of things that cause doubt.
It is mostly represented in a good way of being,
it helps people out, expecially their way of seeing.
I am glad to meet you, glad to see you today,
which give a good expression of things along the way.
The word glad is usually in the positive way for the
    good,
something negative come out, things not being like it
    should.
It represents, feeling joy about something that is right,
hoping that things work for the good and not getting up
    tight.
Being glad is a cause for joy, which is a good way to be,
hoping that things work out, is a good way to see.
It represent making things bright for the beauty of one
    day,
to work in the way of good so peace be the way.
It represent in a way which express willingness to help
    out,
it brings out goodness which bring about a shout.
It is for everything to work for the good for what it
    represent,
that is the outcome of things that is the intent.

13. Grief

Represent a bad way of feeling, a bad way of being,
because of the outcome that way of seeing.
It is the condition of life that come about,
because of what it represent, there is sadness and
doubt.
Grief represent sorrow that a person face now and
then,
it is that part of life that represent things coming to
an end.
Grief is something we go through, which produce
sorrow,
it make a person feel like there is no tomorrow.
That's a part of life that is hard to get use to,
because of what it represent, things being so true.
This matter take a toll on a person from time to time,
it's thing represented in the way, sometime
represented by crime.
It takes time, which represent life as hard to take,
it maybe represented to them as something like a
mistake.
This time of life has a certain affect with things,
because of the outlook of life, the result it brings.

14. Happy

Happy is the expression which show feeling and joy,
that's just like a child who receive a brand new toy.
It represent a person being good by and by,
who receive a gift without a question as to why.
Happy is an expression that represent a good way with
    things,
it is compensation to others and happy it brings.
There are things in life that has a happy ending,
because it represent things in life with a new beginning.
Happy to be around, happy to be here today,
because of the expression of things that make it that
    way.
Happy is something that come from within, coming from
    the heart,
it's like a husband and wife being together and never
    depart.
Happy is like going through life for a contented day,
working for peace, hoping that things continues that
    way.
Happy is knowing that everything works in the way of
    good,
and seeing that everything works like it should.
Happy is trying to work things out to a peaceful resolve,
it is working for good, for everything that involve.
Happy is the best mean to take care of tension and strive,
it is looking at things for the best advice.

15. Humble

Is to know one weakness, knowing what things is about,
to do things in the way that brings a shadow of doubt.
It is a person not acting too proud or bold,
it's a person that respect others and do as they are told.
It's a person that give in to what others has to say,
their main objective is to let peace be the way.
This person knows their own weakness and fault,
they do not act in a way that cause default.
This individual do not consider himself above anybody
    else,
they do not place blame, but take what's left.
He place himself in rank lower than anybody else,
because of how he looks at things he do not praise
    himself.
This person does not take pride in bragging on oneself,
he operates on the efficiency of what he has left.
He do not take things too funny or amusing,
he do not want it to lead to things that are abusing.
Humble is a good way in society that people sometime
    be,
it help out in the way of society for people to see.
Humble is a good way to be in this day and time,
to stay away from things that is associated with crime.

16. Interest

Is the time or way it take to notice things,
because of the good of it the results it brings.
Interest is to show concern for something or look at,
for the good of things, an assessment like that.
It is the consideration that's shown when things may
    come about,
to get to the matter of things so their won't be doubt.
To follow through with, to get something done,
in order to work for good and share the fun.
It is the way that is shown how things may come
    about,
to work for the common interest that would take care
    of doubt.
It's the understanding, the how and the when,
the way one go about things, every now and then.
Interest is taking a shining look that may come
    about,
because of what it represent, for things to work out.
People gain interest from getting an understanding
    of things,
they work in that effort to see what good it brings.

17. Impatient

Is the state of mind, where a person cannot wait,
it does not involve the disciple to last the time it
   take.
It involve the way a person look at things, their state
   of mind,
it's like they try to do something so they won't get
   behind.
It involves a person attitude toward what they do,
trying to hurry things up, trying to rush things threw.
They do not take time to wait in their way of seeing,
that a part of their attitude, their way of being.
In their state of mind, there's no waiting on things,
because of the slow pace and the result it bring.
This person in not too willing to put up with a delay,
they want things to speed up along the way.
This person do not wait for things to come around,
they act like they are in a hurry, that's how things
   are bound.
People are too impatient to wait around for things,
because of the length of time this way brings.
This does not involve taking time to do things right,
but rushing it through somethings might get uptight.
Impatient is a way of life, people often come about,
they do no take proper time to work thing out.

18. Jealous

Jealous is someone who look at things and desire what others got,
because of their way of looking, it affect stability a lot.
It affect their state of mind, their way of seeing,
looking at what others have, their way of being.
Jealous cause people to get mad, to get upset about things,
because of the out look that what jealous brings.
Looking at others, seeing what they have,
not thankful for what they got, whether it's a lot or a dab.
Jealous would affect a person way of life, their state of mind,
it would cause uncertainty in their life, they would find.
Trying to do something somebody else was doing,
it cause uncertainty to their life or cause ruin.
Looking at what others have, looking at their possession,
looking at that way, may lead to obsession.
It would affect a person state of mind, their way of being,
it would cause a person to have heartache in their way of seeing.
Jealous is worrying about someone taking attention from others,
that brings about ill feeling between sister and brother.

19. Joy

Joy is what a person try to acquire out of life,
which would help in the dealing of things like strife.
It would give a person a notion to feel good about,
it takes away those matters that causes a shadow of
doubt.
Joy is an expression that makes a person feel good about
things,
it takes away uncertainty and happiness it brings.
Joy is a very happy feeling that brings about delight,
it helps the dealing of life that makes things up tight.
When a person is joyful, it shown by the expression the
face,
it makes everything seem in order, that everything is in
place.
When a person have joy, they have a better feeling with
things,
they have a better out look, for the good it brings.
Joy makes a person feel at ease during the day,
it take away uncertainty and makes peace the way.
When we have joy, we have a peaceful out look on
things,
it would bring ou sunshine, even when there's rain.
Joy is a good expression of life, it makes a person feel
glad,
it take away the ill feeling, that make a person feel sad.
Jubilation come from joy in the form of celebration,
because of how things are represented in the situation.

20. Kindness

Kindness is when someone do a good deed for another,
to work toward the effort of things for each other.
It is an expression of the way of life that is good,
it makes things turn out in life like it should.
Kindness represent a person who give a helping hand,
they occupy in the way of good so others would
    understand.
Kindness is an expression of a good state of mind,
which is a good way to express oneself, a good way to
    find.
Kindness is giving aid and comfort to someone in
    sorrow,
trying to give a better understanding of tomorrow.
This represent a way that is good, a way that is right,
helping someone out when things are slight.
Kindness is the way that help life, not to be so upset.
it helps take away the things in life that cause regret.
A true and kind word from a person goes a long way,
it help in the out look toward the cheering up of one day.
Kindness is something that come from the heart, come
    from within,
we are to treat a person with kindness, no telling when.
No matter where we go, we are to be kind there,
to do what we know, in kindness we care.

21. Laugh

Is to find something funny and thrilling to laugh about,
this help to enchant things that may cause doubt.
It is a quick reaction, a sound that a person make,
it depends upon humor expression for laughter to take.
Laughter is a expression of joy about how things is said,
that an indication of laughter, how it is made.
That depends upon what is said or how things come
    about,
it is an out burst of sound, sometimes making a shout.
It is the art of bring laughter in a person life,
to help take care of things like tension and strife.
This sometimes enable people to get along with one
    another,
long as it's done in a friendly way and no picking on
    other.
How do a laugh come about, when do a person know
    when,
is it the smile on a person face or is it a grin?
A smile is the first step before a laugh is made,
a grin come about when a little more is said.
When a smile and grin is involve, a laught come about,
when that happens, the expression of a newborn shout.
Laugh is a quick sound of the mouth that come out,
that represent humor or sometime nonsense come about.

22. Manner

Manner is to take care of something that need to be done,
it's done in the way of a group or either by one.
It is the way people go about to put things together,
it depends upon the outcome, sometimes the weather.
When a person's in a good mood, their's a better way with thing,
if they are in a bad mood, uncertainty it may bring.
Manner depends upon the life style, the move one make,
it depends upon the out come or things that are forsake.
Sometime manner is shown in an angry way,
sometime it's shown for good that speaks for that day.
People need to be careful toward there work with things,
to work toward the good for the best manner it brings.
Sometimes a person manner can lead them to danger,
they sometime express themselves like a stranger.
Sometimes people have a shameful manner, that way with things,
they do not care what they do, the result it brings.
Sometimes a person has a mischievous manner of causing harm,
they do things in a way that causes alarm.

23. Nice

Nice is a person who represent the way of good,
it's the attitude of a person, where things go like it
should.
It represents a good way, a person being kind,
because of the outcome that one would find,
This represent a person being good and kind during the
day,
this representation of things in a peaceful way.
It also represent good people that is around,
to work for the order of things that is sound.
Being nice among people, helps put things at ease,
it goes in the order of things that is please.
This is a representation of peace where good comes out,
this make things go, where good come about.
The expression of being nice enables people to see
things clear,
they are an expression of themselves, they call each
other dear.
Being nice treating the other person with respect,
doing things in a way that do not cause regret.
How nice could a person be for things to be this way,
according to understanding, not nice enough for peace
always.

24. Outrage

It is the representation of things in a cruel and evil way,
it may cause hardship to the future of one day.
Outrage is the way of things that lead to disgust,
they act in a way that people would not trust.
People acting in outrage is a bad way to be,
when things reach that point, peace is hard to see.
This represent things, that is shocking and wickness,
it brings about things that may cause sickness.
It is the environment that brings on angry,
if things reach a certain point, there is danger.
Outrage is a dangerous situation for things to be,
because of how it affect people like you and me.
Because of the affect of outrage that state of mind,
it brings on more difficult and make things hard to find.
In this state of mind, it's hard for one to find themselves,
when it reach that point, it's hard to find anyone else.
War itself is an outrage that cause harm to mankind,
because of the destruction it cause and leave behind.
It leave behind pain and agony, an expression on people
    face,
it cause destruction which is an outrage toward disgrace.

25. Uncertain

Uncertain means not sure of how things are going to go,
because of the out look, nobody actually know.
Here are uncertainty in life that cause doubt,
because of that way of looking that's how things work
   out.
Sometime we do not know how things are going in life,
whether or not it's following the right order or strife.
Sometime in life we are not certain of what to do,
because of the direction, don't know which way is true.
Sometimes we can go down one road, and it lead to a
   dead end,
go down another road and wonder where did it begin.
It is that kind of uncertainty that give understanding in
   life,
not to be too sure of things because of the strife.
Uncertain play a part in our life, making us think twice,
to slow down with things to get good advice.
Sometime we do not know th right way to go,
we would inquire about things until we know.
Uncertain is a path of life that we are not too sure about,
being of the situation of things that bring on doubt.
This is the certain of matters that need attention,
because of the situation of things that need to be
   mention.

26. Value

The value in life, how do things work out,
the value of things, what is it all about.
How do we look at it, how do we asset things,
how do we look at it for the result it brings?
How do we look at the value of things in this day and
    time,
Is ten cent the true value of a dime?
Our value in life depends upon our belief and ideal,
it represents those things in life that are precious and
    real.
Sometime the value go up, and sometime it goes down,
that depends on the situation of things and how it is
    bound.
How do we instill value into our way of thinking,
we hold onto what we got, so morality won't start
    sinking.
As we look at things, what is the value of life,
it is to represent peace without tension and strife.
How do we go about determining the value of things,
is it represented in the way of good or is there a gains.
More value in life, would come by a positive insight,
doing that which is good, doing that which is right.
To determine how we look at things, how we conduct
    our self,
take this same care and concern to other, on the right our
    left.

27. Waver

Show uncertain in a certain way of being,
this mood is reflected to others in their way of seeing.
Acting in a manner not sure of how things go about,
because of that way of acting, brings out certain doubt.
This would catch the attention of others being around,
looking at the uncertainty, how things may be bound.
When a person waver, they're not sure of the decision
they make,
they don't know the aim of things, whether or not it's a
mistake.
They try to sort things through, to do the best they can,
they do not have a clear picture so they understand.
Wavers can mean to flutter before something go out,
this would give a clear understanding of what this is
about.
Waver can mean to quiver, as like not to stand still,
this would not follow the order of thing according to
one's will.
It also means tremble, which has the same way of being,
quiver or tremble, duplicate, according to one's way of
seeing.
A candle light can waver just before it goes out,
it represent the shadow of darkness, about to come
about.
When a person wavers, they're not too sure of what's
going on,
they do not know how to determine things, whether right
or wrong.

Analysis of Tomorrow

1. From a singer's perspective

If I could see tomorrow, I would sing a special song
Thinking about tomorrow, as time goes along.
Looking at tomorrow, the tune I would sing,
Thinking of a peaceful outlook, the joy it bring.
Singing a song, if I could see tomorrow,
It would help the joy of life, to deal with the sorrow.
Looking at tomorrow for the peace of thing,
What must we do for this tune we sing.
If I could see tomorrow, I would shape the world
    like this,
Take away some of the uncertain, that cause risk.

2. From a person who try to find themselves

If I could see tomorrow, where would I be?
Would I be doing the things that pleasing to thee?
Looking at tomorrow for the peace of things,
Would I be contented, that way it brings?
If I could see tomorrow, how would I treat others?
Would I treat them like my sisters and brothers?
Looking at tomorrow, how things would be,
Would there be peace and joy, for everybody to see.

3. From a selfish person's perspective

If I could see tomorrow, how would I be?
Would I treat everybody the way I treat me?
Looking at tomorrow and the order of things
Are we to do right, for peace it brings?
Looking at tomorrow, the way things may be,
Would I be doing right for the world to see?
Things are different, than the way it used to be.
There are less respect in the world to see.
Because of today world, different result of things,
If I could see tomorrow, what would it bring?

4. From a Christian person's perspective

If I could see tomorrow, how would things be?
Would it be in the way of good, that we see?
We need to do something about the world we are
   living in.
If I could see tomorrow, what then?
If I could see tomorrow, I may do things different
   somehow,
But it always come back to today, the time is now.
Thank God that we have a tomorrow to look forward
   to.
Without Jesus, what in the world would we do?
Looking at tomorrow, and the time we are living in,
Let's pray for the good so peace happens within.

5. From a person who tries to do right

If I could see tomorrow, what could I do?
Stand for the right so God blessing would come thru.
The question one ask, what will tomorrow bring?
With God anything possible, perhaps sunshine or rain.
Our tomorrow depend upon what we do today.
Are we following the order of things, God's way?
If I could see tomorrow, what would I do today?
Follow the order of things in God we obey.
If I could see tomorrow, how would I act?
Would things be in order, or be out of tact.
If I could see tomorrow, what a day that would be.
Thank God for Jesus, who made us free.
Thinking about Jesus what He done for me
He open our eyes, He cause the blind to see.

6. From a child's perspective

If I could see tomorrow, what would I see?
Thinking about tomorrow, where would I be?
If I could see tomorrow, what would I know?
Thinking about tomorrow, where would I go?
If I could see tomorrow, what would I do?
Thinking about tomorrow, how about you?
If I could see tomorrow, what would things be?
Looking at tomorrow, would I be closer to thee?
If I could see tomorrow, what would I expect?
Would things be right or that we reject?
If I could see tomorrow, how would things be received?
Would it be by what we say or that we believe?
If I could see tomorrow, how would things be looked at?
Would it be more out of order, or more in tact?
If I could see tomorrow, what would the future bring?
Would it be something different or the same old thing?
If I could see tomorrow, how would children behave?
Would it be more like the parent guidance they presuave?
If I could see tomorrow, how different would be thing?
With the hope of tomorrow, what would the future bring?
If I could see tomorrow, what would I see?
If I could see tomorrow, how would things be?
If I could see tomorrow, where would I go?
If I could see tomorrow, what place would I know?
If I could see tomorrow, where would I be?
If I could see tomorrow, how would things be with me?
If I could see tomorrow, what shape would the world be in?
How would things be tomorrow, how would it be then?

7. From a confused person's perspective

If I could see tomorrow, I see the world a differetn way.
Looking at tomorrow, what would I do different today?
If I could see tomorrow, tell me what the world would be;
Looking at tomorrow, tell me what I would see.
If I could see tomorrow, I would sing a special song.
Looking at tomorrow as time goes along.
If I could see tomorrow, what kind of world would it be?
Thinking about tomorrow, would we be more or less free?
If I could see tomorrow, how would things appear?
Looking at the future of tomorrow, time so dear.

8. From a teenager's perspective

If I could see tomorrow, would things be out of bound?
How would life be tomorrow, would it be upside down?
What must we do, to help the generation of tomorrow?
What must we do to help in their pain and sorrow?
There are uncertain in life that are found.
There are situations that cause things to get out of
    bound.
What would I do if I could see tomorrow?
Would I be better person, would there be less sorrow?
Looking at tomorrow, what would the future bring?
Would there be more peace, or the same old thing?

9. From an average person's perspective

If I could see tomorrow, what would I expect?
Looking at things, that are good, or that which cause upset.
Looking at tomorrow, where would the future be at?
Would there be an assetment of good, things like that?
Looking at tomorrow, where would the future be?
Would there be things of bad, more than we see?
What could I do if I could see tomorrow?
Would I add to the good, or add to the sorrow?
Thinking about tomorrow, what would the future be?
If we do what right, we would be closer to thee.

10. From a college person's perspective

If I could see tomorrow, how would things be?
Would things be impossible or hard to see?
Looking at tomorrow how things work out.
Would it be toward good or that which cause doubt?
Looking at tomorrow, how things are before us,
Can we depend upon other, in the way we trust?
Looking at tomorrow, what the future would bring,
What must we do, to enhant the way of thing?
The generation of today, that represent the future do.
Looking at tomorrow, trying to see the good for the best.
Trying to work things out, toward the way of success.

11. From a parent's perspective

The future is tomorrow, what must we do?
To work for a better outlook, to make things true.
Let's look at tomorrow from what we do today,
To work for the peace of things, to work for a better way.
Looking at tomorrow, the way things suppose to be,
What can we do for the good, that people can see?
Looking at tomorrow, from the way of things we expect,
Knowing that which is good, and that we reject.
Thinking about tomorrow, where would our mind be?
Would it be on the things that are pleasing to thee?

12. From a woman's perspective

Looking at tomorrow the time it would bring,
Would it be something different or the same old thing?
If we could see tomorrow, to project what the future hold,
Would things in life be more careful or more bold?
Looking at tomorrow, looking at what ahead,
Would we be more careful in life or easy lead?
How must we look at life as things appear?
Would this give us a better meaning of the word called fear?
Looking at tomorrow, what can we expect?
Would there be more delight or things get upset?
Looking at the future, and what the future hold,
Would things get better, children do more as they told?

13. From a spiritual family's perspective

Thinking about the Gospel, that is manifest from above;
It was given by Jesus, through in by his love.
Looking at tomorrow, through a child would normal be.
If they would determine tomorrow, through their parent
    they would see.
Looking at tomorrow, as time goes along.
It would determine tomorrow, how they would sing a
    song.
Looking at tomorrow, what would a child know?
They must follow the guidance of their parent, the way
    they go.
Children are placed with others their age in school,
They are to gain learning in life and obey the rules.
If I could see tomorrow, how would things be ahead?
Would uncertain in life continue to spread?

14. From a future singer's perspective

Looking at tomorrow, what the future would bring;
If I could see tomorrow, what tune would I sing?
Talking about tomorrow the way that I make.
It would determine the aim of life, the step that I take.
Looking at tomorrow, the time we are living in,
What must we do, for more peace to be within?
Take it to Jesus, he would show us the way;
Take it to Jesus, he would brighten up our day.
As we look at tomorrow, seeing how things transpire,
There are questions that may come about, and a reason
   as to why.
If I could see tomorrow, I see the world a different way.
Looking at tomorrow, depend upon what I do today.

15. From a judge's perspective

We are looking at a change, not only in the way of time.
There are much to say about the way of crime.
Looking at tomorrow, there are certain doubt that come
    about;
Seeing how things go, hoping that things work out.
Looking at the future, the world we must face,
If things do not change, there are certain disgrace;
Looking at the world, the time that upon us.
If we do not straighten out, there would be disgust.
What must we do, for tomorrow to bring a change?
If we could see tomorrow, would there be a peaceful
    gain:
Thinking about the situation, how things in life come
    about.
What must we do in life, to take care of the doubt?

16. From a police perspective

There are things in life, that cause disgust.
These are the things in life, that we do not trust.
Looking at the matter of life, how things may be
    involved.
There are problems in life, that we need to solve.
If I could see tomorrow, how would things be?
Would there be less good in life, for us to see?
Looking at the situation and how things may come
    about,
Are we doing all we can to take care of the doubt?
There is confusion and mix up in life to see,
That cause uncertain in life, for things to be.

17. From a minister's perspective

Looking at the confusion in life, for things to be
    involved;
That bring about more difficult in life, for things to be
    solved.
If we could see tomorrow, what must we do?
We must stay in the Word of God, and then be true.
If we could see tomorrow, how would things be for us?
To stay in the Word of God, in him we can trust.
How must we look at tomorrow, for what the future
    bring?
Shall we look for something different or the same old
    thing?
How must we see tomorrow for what the future bring?
How must we see tomorrow, for the different tune we
    sing?

The ABC of School Sports

1. Baseball

Baseball is a game that adult and children play.
It helps them pass the time of day.
It occupies their mind, it gives them something to do.
It's a game of life that makes dreams come true.
This game is usually played on a beautiful day.
Two teams against one another, in a peaceful way;
Trying to get points for their side the best they can,
Doing it in a way, that everybody would understand.
Baseball is a game on the outside, only people play.
It is done for togetherness, to help make peace the way.

A is for another player at bat trying to hit the ball;
B is for batter hitting, whether short or tall;
C is for catcher, catching the ball behind the plate;
D is for dugout, where the players sit and wait;
E is for education, for the understanding of the game;
F is for fair play, hoping everybody do the same;
G is for great play, at that time of day;
H is for hoping everything would continue that way;
I is for infield, that player effort that involved in a
   double play;
J is for joy that is received that time of day;
K is for kick that this game give as a boost to life;
L is for love that this game offer to help take care of
   strife;
M is for manager, the one who manages the team of the
   game;
N is for nine active players who sign their name;
O is for occupation of this game, that brought to the
   people attention;
P is for pay of the player, that is sometime mention;
Q is for quest of the game, that broadens people's
   perspective;
R is for remember of the game, its history and objective;

S is for section, the place that determine one team from another;

T is for team player in the game trying to beat the other;

U is for unity that team players share during this time;

V is for victory that brings the game to its height and prime;

W is for winning which represent in part what the game is about;

X is for symbol X which represent three strikes as out;

Y is for you, who could possibly become a baseball player too;

Z is for zeroing on one dream, who may one day become true.

2. Basketball

Basketball is a game involving the bouncing of the ball.
Different players play, some short, some tall.
They bounce the ball, to their goal to score,
To see whose points, add up to be more.
The game involves determination and skill;
It also involves a degree of one's will.
People come from all around to support the game,
Hoping one day someone would achieve fame.

A is for around to each team end, the distance is the same.

B is for bouncing the ball to score in the game.

C is for coaching the game that determines the score.

D is for doing right, being fair to both teams on the floor.

E is for ekoh, the way the players sometimes play.

F is for foul play, how things turn out that way.

G is for great play, how things sometimes come about.

H is for hoping that things continue to work out.

I is for involvement that the team share on the court.

J is for joy that continues to come from this sport.

K is for kindness and consideration shown in the sport.

L is for lending the ball to the other members on the court.

M is for movement of the ball as it travels about.

N is for national involvement of the game, how things work out.

O is for outlook of the game, how it national involve.

P is for plans that bring the game to this resolve.

Q is for quest and involvement that sometimes comes about.

R is for remember of profession that sometimes work out.

S is for seating arrangement that is made before the game play.

T is for tension and action, how things sometime work that way.

U is for up and underneath which represents seating arrangement.

V is for victory which gives a definite understanding of how the game went.

W is for the way things may sometimes come about.

X is for xerox which represent the way things may work out.

Y is for yourself, who may one day be a basketball player too.

Z is for zoning in on things, that may make dreams come true.

3. Football

Football is one of the most roughest sports around;
It sometimes causes accident is how things is bound,
Trying to get to the other end, to make a touchdown.
Quite often people find themselves on the ground,
Going after the ball, sometimes scrambling around,
Putting up a defense, a trying to push the other person
down.
Because of the action, that how the game go,
people need to be careful, because of the danger they
know.
This game deals with two sides against one another,
Trying to keep the ball for their side from the other.

A is for advantagement of the football on the field.
B is for backing of the play, stopping the advantage and
not yield.
C is for coaching that gives the player knowledge of the
play.
D is for doing it right the first time, that the way.
E is for entertainment of the play, that was made.
F is for following the instruction, what the coach has
said.
G is for gaining knowledge and understanding of what's
going on.
H is for height of the matter, getting it right and not
wrong.
I is for initiative of the play how things is said.
J is for jointing the right effort, how things is made.
K is for kicking the football, in order to make a field
goal.
L is for looking out for the other player, to do what one
know.
M is for management of the play, to see that things go
right.

N is for nearing the opponent line, while things may get tight.

O is for outlook that involve the procedure of the game.

P is for planning the outcome, in order to achieve fame.

Q is for quest toward the knowledge of the game.

R is for remember the circumstance, people could become hurt or lame.

S is for school that has such a rugged sport as this.

T is for taking a closer look at things that involve risk.

U is for unity of player, that is involve in the game.

V is for Victory, how things is achieve and attain.

W is for winning, everybody starting out with the same ideal.

X is for extra excitement, when this ideal become real.

Y is for you, the involvement of this game that cause hurt joint.

Z is for zone, the achievement someone may acquire from this point.

4. Wrestling

Wrestling is a sport that requires strength and speed.
They are in a tussing match, mostly not with ease.
They might have a tough time, a tough time to go.
Each opponent trying to show the other, what they know.
It's a tussing match, they trying to do the best they can.
It requires the movement of the feet, and the shifting of the hand.
Each opponent standing from the other face to face.
Trying to see what they can do, to get the other out of place.
The object of the sport, is to go for the pin.
When that is accomplished, that person win.

A is for attitude, the degree for a person to hold their own.
B is for build or determination to show they are strong.
C is for concentration for a person's alertness to what they are doing.
D is for determination, so they know how things are going.
E is for effort because for the time a person put in.
F is for following through to put the other person in a pin.
G is for guard against being taken down on the match.
H is for hoping not to be taken down by a body snatch.
I is for involvement of the effort that is put out.
J is for jaking and fast movement, so a win would come about.
K is for keep eyes on the opponent and watching his move.
L is for looking out, and not to be caught in a groove.
M is for movement in a match, that involve wrestling and tussing.

N is for no negativity that may lead to fussing.

O is for outlook that lead to a good resolve.

P is for positive ways, because of how things involve.

Q is for quest or determination it take on or off the floor.

R is for remember it take determination even something more.

S is for surrounding one determination, one state of mind.

T is for talent to hold on and not get behind.

U is for uniform effort it take to put one in a body snatch.

V is for victory the effort it take in winning the match.

W is for winning when the loser of the match is pin.

X is for extra and determination, when the match come to an end.

Y is for your effort, which is put out trying to win.

Z is for zero start, the time the match begin.

5. Vollyball

Volleyball involve the ball going to both side of the net.
The ball go that way, for things to be set.
The ball go across the net to and fro.
The object of the game, to see who get the best score.
Each try to knock the ball on the other team's side;
Trying to keep the ball in play, so the score would abide.
The objective of the game is to keep the ball on other side of net.
Trying to do the best they can, to see what point they get.
Trying to spike the ball, hit it every kind of way.
To out maneuver the opponent, to bet them that day.

A is for above the net, so the ball would not land.
B is for bouncing not to be done, but by hitting of the hand.
C is for coaching the ball up, hitting it by one another.
D is for doing your best, so it won't be gotten by the other.
E is for energy that is involved to play the game.
F is for follow-through so the ball would not be attain.
G is for gaining understanding and knowledge of volleyball.
H is for hoping on the outset, that it would not fall.
I is for involvement that involve in hitting the ball.
J is for jumping to make point, where short or tall.
K is for kind of activity that involve hitting the ball over net.
L is for leaping up and down after winning the game set.
M is for managing the game from beginning to end.
N is for not being proud of things, unless there's a win.
O is for occurrance within the game, how it made.
P is for planning within the game, how things is said.
Q is for quest and the understanding of the game.

R is for remember things, would not remain the same.
S is for sound and notice of how things is made.
T is for taking notes of everything done and said.
U is for unity and an understanding of the game itself.
V is for victory only one team win and nobody else.
W is for winning is why people try to do that.
X is for xerox, to get an assetment of how things is at.
Y is for your understanding of what the game is about.
Z is for zoning in on the prospective of how things may
    work out.

6. Tennis

Tennis is a game with a ball and racket played by two.
Each player on their side of net, seeing what they can do.
They hit the ball to each side of the net.
Trying to see who win the game, who win the set.
Trying to move their opponent around, the best they can.
They do this by powerful swing, even a power backhand.
Hoping to hit the ball by their opponent to score.
Try to see who can add up the point 6 or more.
Each player move their opponent all around the court.
That bring excitement to the fan, and give more to the sport.

A is for attitude, a person state of mind on the tennis court.
B is for balance and speed that bring out the pace of this sport.
C is for carefulness of trying to hit the ball all around.
D is for determination of trying to get the other player out of bound.
E is for effort, the time spent on the court.
F is for following through with the cheering of the sport.
G is for gaining experience, that involves playing the game.
H is for hoping with the ideal, that one may achieve fame.
I is for initiative that if involve to win the set.
J is for jubilation that come from knocking an ace over the net.
K is for kinetic energy that require from begin to end.
L is for long jeopardy that help a person to win.
M is for mation and movement, that help take care of the doubt.
N is for non-stop which add up to a person holding out.

O is for outcome of things, which add to the benefit.

P is for payment and prestige, that one gain from it.

Q is for quest that is made when a person act like they not tame.

R is for remembering the sportsmanship, that involve in this game.

S is for sound a person made, while sometime hitting the ball.

T is for taking notice of a person, whether short or tall.

U is for understanding that involve the significant of the game.

V is for victory that is won, once that is attain.

W is for winning of the game to its peak, for people to stand.

X is for extra ability that involve both women and men.

Y is for you and another player, playing the game on the court.

Z is for zoning in on target, which bring out the ecstasy of the sport.

A

another -   Another way to look at things, to get the best advice.
             To seek for help, to deal with the strive.

around -   Around for the good, is a good purpose for being
             around.   To help aid things, in the right way its
             bound.

advantage - Trying to move toward the advantage point, So that
             things would be right, and not out of joint.

altitude -   This word is mostly determine in a negative way. It
             act out by a person action, with not much good to
             say.

above -   is for determine of the fact of things that is above.
             To look at the one in charge, God and his love.

B

balance -   Is to achieve a person and meaning in one life, To
             keep things as even as possible to limit strife.

backing -   Is to give assure and help people, who need a hand.
             But do it in a way, that everybody would understand.

build -   To build a character, an understanding of what
             things is about. In order to deal with problem, that
             may cause doubt.

bouncing - Is the movement of things up and down, But do it in
             a way so uncertain won't be around.

C

catch - To catch up with knowledge and understanding of things. To pay more attention better understanding it brings.

concentration - Careful of one action, how things is going around. So one know how to look at things, in the way its bound.

carefulness - Be careful in one expression along the way. To help determine the best outcome of the day.

carrying - Is for carrying oneself and altitude in a responsible way. To work for peace, to help determine the outcome of the day.

coaching - Being on the look-out for one attention of commanding. Doing what right to acquire understanding.

D

doing - Is the process of something happen, as things going along. It is determine by that which is right or wrong.

determination – Is the devotion and altitude to see things through. The degree which determine what a person can do.

E

Education - Is the knowledge and requirement that gain in school. Which involve following the procedure, following the rule.

112

effort - Is that which is put forward, that involve one determination. To assert the understanding of things even the situation.

energy - Is that which is put forward, during an active time of day. To help one to be active, for things to be that way.

F

fair play - Involve peace, understanding and the best way with things. To work for the right, is the best result it brings.

foul play - Deal with confusion and mix up for things to come about. Which deal with unfairness, that cause things to be in doubt.

following - Following through with things, is the right way to go. Doing that which is right, is the right way we know.

G

gaining knowledge - Is for gaining knowledge and understanding of what going on. Doing what is right, so things won't be wrong.

gaining experience - Gaining experience of the game, the way things going on. Doing what is right, so things won't be wrong.

guard - Guard against ill, the things which affect life. Do what is right, so it won't bring on tension and strife.

H

hoping -   Hoping to get an understanding, hoping to do it right. To do things in the manner, that would not become uptight.

height -   Is reaching to the highest point, the best one can go. Following the order of things, the best one know.

I

involvement -   Is the way of things that is involve. It is the degree it take to make things solve.

initiative -   It is the response that people take to do things. If it is guilded by good, positive result it brings.

J

joy -   Joy represent peace for thing to be that way. It determine the outcome, the happiness of one day.

jointing -   Is for jointing in to help out with the effort of things. It represent working together for the best result it brings.

jubilation -   It is the representation of joy, express during an event. A gathering of peace and happiness it represent.

jumping -   Jumping toward the cause of things which is right. Do not jump in a way, that would cause a fight.

Is something that does not work positive is the result it brings.

K

kick - Is the expression one say, they get a kick out of things. But do not misunderstand the meaning it brings.

kindness - Is the expression, on welcome to come about. Happiness is what it represent, it cause no doubt.

kinetic - Is the energy which help people to move along. It help them in activity that make them seem strong.

L

love - Is express in a way that show concern for one another. It represent a way that show love for the other.

looking - Represent looking at the future, looking ahead. Looking at the best outcome, so things won't be dread.

leaping - Represent leaping into the future, leaping about. Looking at the best outcome, for things to work out.

M

manager - Represent managing one business, how one go about things. Doing that which is right, for the best it brings.

movement - Represent the movement of things, how one go about their way. Which determine the process, whether work or play.

N

nine player - Represent the number of active players on each team. They go to the game with confident, so they have self-esteem.

national involvement - is the team in the big league with national attention. They gain that status in life, because they are well mention.

negativity - Is that which give a negative response to things.net – Represent the real money after the gross amount. Which is that you can spend, the money you can count.

non-stop - Is the motion that is given, when one continue on. To determine the outlook of things, how things goes along.

O

occupation - Is the work one acquire to have a positive outlook on life. It help take care of money matters, that lead to strife.

outlook - Is the way one try to acquire a positive understanding. Try to stick with that which is good, and not that which is demanding.

occurrance - Is something which occur within a define period of time. It depend upon the happen, it may not always be a crime.

outcome - The degree or way, that determine how things work out. It is the determination of the way, how things come about.

P

pay - Is receipt of payment given for a job that was done. It may be boring or it may sometime be fun.

plan - Is to look ahead for things, in the future sight. To do that which is good, that which is right.

positive - Is looking at things in a good outcome, a good way. This would help determine the future of one day.

Q

quest - Is that which we seek for the benefit of good. To do that which is right and hope things work like it should.

R

remember - Is to look at things in history, to look at the past. To look at the accomplishment, and hope that it last.

racket - Is that which is used to hit the tennis ball. To acquire an understanding, so on the other side it fall.

S

section - Is that which different, on way from another. To get an understanding, a different from the other.

seating - Is the arrangement of seating mode, whether people gather. It done for the purpose under the roof, in spite the weather.

school - Is a place where one gain knowledge and understanding. It is that way because thing in the world, is more demanding.

surround - We surround ourselve in the right environment, right way to be Because of the process of life, that would make things free.

sound - Is the matter that determine the noise in situation like game. It is the situation the calling out loud of one name.

T

team - Is the member or group, who try to win a game. They try to beat the others, who trying to do the same.

tension - Is frustration that come, when things do not work out. It cause uncertain in life, even more doubt.

taking - It represent taking advantage of duty and responsible giving. This is for everybody, who represent the living.

talent - Is that which a person do, that make things turn out good. It is represented in the way of top performance, how things should.

U

unity - It represent working together, for something on a common call. It represent working together for one, and working together for all.

up and underneath - Represent the place that someone would go at. To get a understanding of things, an assetment like that.

understanding - Is the ability to think, the ability to reason things out. To know something for sure, and without a doubt.

V

victory -   Is winning performance that made after a game. It represent the noise of cheering, other people doing the same.

About the Author

Larry W. McEachin was born in Hoke County, North Carolina. I lived there from the time that I was born. I am 47 years old. I have been a shy person for most of my life. Writing this book was a form of therapy for me. Along with the help of the Holy Spirit, I wrote a poem book that would inspire, encourage, and motivate a person the right way with things. If a person is feeling bad and down, my book will lift their spirit and make them feel better about themself. That's why I wrote this book: to help people out with their feelings in a positive way. This is my first book.